presents

My Leap of Faith Journal

By:

_____

Leap of faith.

What does that mean?

Leap: to throw oneself headlong into the unknown, or to skip over. There's a choice.

Faith: to believe in…something. What?

Diana Lyn Cote

For me, the leap was not to skip over, but to throw myself blindly into a year of exploration that, as it turned out, actually opened my eyes. It began with the simple question asked by Anne Kubitsky in the beginning of 2012: What makes you grateful? Hmmmm. It ended up as a journey of 366 days, a leap year. Each day revealed small insights into what was clearly directing me to the bigger picture. The answer, I found, is just as simple as the question. It comes from the highest and most humble of sources and is completely available to all of us: that is gratitude. And it is, oddly, a choice.

I believe that the outer world in which we live is created by the world we each construct inside our own mind. My faith lies in the idea that to change our world we need only change our mind about the world. Focusing the mind to be present in the space of each moment, to appreciate it, and then to let it go is our connection with everything. The moment is brief, and then it is gone, though not lost if we've given ourselves fully to it. I wholeheartedly believe if you look for the good, you will not only find it, you will create it.

So, I invite you to enjoy this selection of paintings as you begin your own journey into gratitude. Watch carefully to the change that will undoubtedly occur just by taking a leap. In that I have great faith.

- Diana Lyn Cote

To take YOUR leap of faith, write in this journal...

When you're feeling grateful;
When you're feeling sad;

Even when you're angry.

Let whatever experience you're having lead you
to love because, deep down, that's all there is.

Life, love, humility, strength...
there is so much to be grateful for.

Can you take a moment to find it?
Let Diana's paintings light the way.

The Look for the Good Project

is a growing collection of grateful thoughts from people around the world organized by project founder, Anne Kubitsky. Since October 2011, Anne has received thousands of messages from all over the world, hosted a variety of exhibits and installations, created a few books... and has unexpectedly gone through a lot of healing.

To learn more about the project and how you can participate, please visit:

www.lookforthegoodproject.org

"Listen to your dreams. You'll realize that taking the big leap or deep dive are never as scary as your waking self wants you to believe."

-Natalie Banker
Project Participant

I am grateful for...

"T-ssssss..... did you hear it?"
- Diana Lyn Cote

I am grateful for...

"I'm imagining what concert the Black-eyed Susans have gathered around the gazebo to hear."

- Diana Lyn Cote

I am grateful for...

"Great presence can also be found in such an ephemeral and diminutive form."
- Diana Lyn Cote

I am grateful for...

"The storm lingers leaving a paled reflection of nature's might."
- Diana Lyn Cote

I am grateful for...

"Each sunset bid its farewell by taking my breath and giving me unquestionable inspiration."
- Diana Lyn Cote

I am grateful for...

I am grateful for...

"Paradise begins and ends in the mind. It can be created anywhere."
- Diana Lyn Cote

I am grateful for...

"Clouds and fields of dry stalks accept the wind's invitation to dance."
- Diana Lyn Cote

I am grateful for...

"Somehow the shoji screen of leaves and powdered white transformed this birch tree into a Geisha's slight bow of humility."
- Diana Lyn Cote

I am grateful for...

"Sunset on the docks in Boston made for a magical evening of dancing, friends, and just being engaged in life."
— Diana Lyn Cote

I am grateful for...

I am grateful for...

"It is surprising how many terms exist for moments of a new day; astrological dawn, nautical dawn, civil dawn, solar dawn, pre-dawn, dawn, morning twilight, and oh yes, sunrise. I prefer not to name it but simply breathe it in."
- *Diana Lyn Cote*

I am grateful for...

I am grateful for...

You are invited to write or draw a glimmer of gladness on a postcard-sized anything and mail it to:

WHAT I'M GRATEFUL FOR
PO BOX 602
Old Lyme, CT 06371
USA

Don't worry, stick figures are perfectly acceptable and you don't have to be *l'artiste*.

To see more postcards, check out:

lookforthegoodproject.org

To learn more about Diana Lyn Cote, please visit:

dianalyncote.com

Made in the USA
Lexington, KY
28 December 2013